# LINES OF SANITY

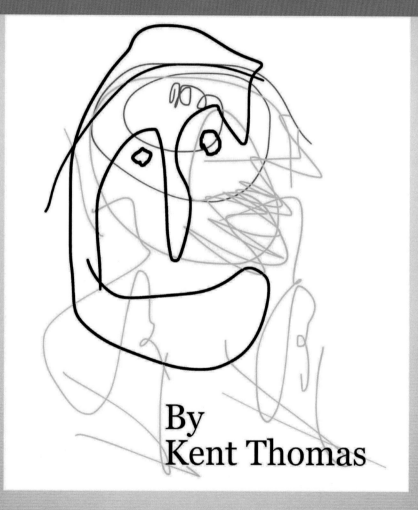

By
Kent Thomas

## True Confessions
## Of A Self~Realized Soul

To order additional copies of this book, contact:
Xlibris
1-888-795-4274
www.Xlibris.com
Orders@Xlibris.com

Editor: Daryl Haley

ISBN:   Softcover      978-1-7960-6278-6
        Hardcover      978-1-7960-6279-3
        EBook          978-1-7960-6277-9

Library of Congress Control Number: 2019915260

Print information available on the last page

Rev. date: 10/15/2019

# LINES OF SANITY

## TRUE CONFESSIONS OF A SELF-REALIZED SOUL

-------------------------

Kent Thomas

Dedicated to my beloved Guru
Paramahansa Yogananda

## Personal Acknowledgments

In 1973, I first saw the value of presenting poetry with artistic considerations when I read the poetic classic by Bernard Gunther, **What To Do Till The Messiah Comes.** \* Then in 2016, I met Pat Parisian who helped me to see the heart of a poet inside my soul. Later that year, I had the pleasure    of meeting the gifted artist, Kent Corban who encouraged me to see through my artistic eye.    In addition, I am eternally grateful to both, Brother Balanananda and Brahmachari Lynn, as I learned from both of them how fast I can flap my broken wings. Most of all, I thank my Guru, **Paramahansa Yogananda**, for **His** guiding light that showed me how to find the **Spirit Of Christ** within myself, allowing me to get closer to **GOD** then I ever imaged.

\* **What To Do Till The Messiah Comes** by Bernard Gunther , © 1971 First Collier Books, The Macmillan Company

## The Noble New* — Paramahansa Yogananda

Sing songs none have sung,

Think thoughts that ne'er in brain have rung,

Walk in paths that none have trod,

Weep tears as none have shed for God,

Give peace to all to whom none other gave,

Claim him your own who's everywhere disclaimed.

Love all the love that none have felt, and brave the battle of life with strength unchained.

* From **Self-Realization Fellowship Lessons**: published by permission of **Self-Realization Fellowship.**

# Contents

## COMMOTION

# LONELINESS

# PAIN AND SUFFERING

# WHAT THE WORLD NEEDS NOW

# FORWARD

James(Pat) W. Parisian, MD

We live in a time of disconnection, disunity and media overload. Materialism, consumerism and sense gratification have become our new religion.This has led to widespread insecurity, dissatisfaction and unhappiness. In spite of our technological advances and material wealth, the world has become a dystopia when it should be a utopia. There is a confusion about the purpose of life and the turmoil we see around us. How can we find peace and serenity? Where should we look for a purpose and fulfillment? It is good to be reminded that this world is not our home. In fact, as scriptures of the east and quantum mechanics attest, this world isn't even real. It is essentially waves of thought and energy with little no real underlying substance.

In **Lines of Sanity**, Kent Thomas has found words and images to inspire a new perspective and a spiritual understanding that gives hope for a more meaningful and peaceful way of life. A new generation, and perhaps an old one too, will find solace in the transformative changes that Kent has observed in his life story as he presents it through poetry and powerful imagery. Kent's deeply felt spiritual connection to the teachings of **Paramahansa Yogananda** will hopefully lead more people to embrace the message of scientific yoga meditation and look within to find the "peace that surpasseth understanding". The great Master often quoted this prayer from the Upanishads: " lead us from the unreal to the real, from the darkness to the light, from death to immortality". Hopefully, **Lines of Sanity** will help to lead many to the realization of these eternal truths.

## Introduction

As individuals travel in daily life, we are subjected to many distractions and pressure from both intrinsic and extrinsic sources. Whether it is pain, disease, or loneliness from within oneself, or the pressures one must endure that present in every day life, especially in this fast paced world, it is easy for one to become lost in these illusions that are found everywhere. One can discover a way to walk the path to find oneself by getting closer to what is truly real in all with **God's** love and the joy with the **Spirit of Christ**. By going within oneself in deep meditation, the individual can find true meaning and oneness with **God**, and from this Self-realization, find peace, love and joy in **God's** light in "**The Daily Fight.**"

We can all benefit from a guide along this journey. **The Master** can guide us along this path but it is up to the individual to make that determination and decide if the illusions are **their** truth. This is a book of poetry and art of a traveler on the journey of this GRAND ILLUSION, finding the **Light of God** from within himself in harmony, with love and guidance from **The Master**.

While there are many different ways of meditating, there is a method that was developed by using long lost techniques from the spiritual mecca of the Himalayas. These techniques were brought to the west by **Paramahansa Yogananda**, the author of the classical best seller, the **Autobiography Of A Yogi** and founder of the world wide religion, Self-Realization Fellowship*. This **Master** has shared with the world the advanced yoga meditation of various techniques, including the most dynamic method, **Kriya yoga**. It is with the practice of these methods that a keen sense of awareness of **God** can start to be developed within all souls. However, it is up to the individual to possess the love, desire and devotion to find this path to **God**.

These methods, along with proper life style and prayer, can result in the development of a harmonious spirit with all who follow this path into the battle of the constant conflagration of modern life. It is then, the preservation of the individual can be achieved with love and understanding along the **Master 's** path to find **God**.

---

*Contact information on page 49.

# PREAMBLE:

# THE NIGHT OF THE ROSES

from the night of the roses the traveler comes
a spirit of freedom with the

**Holy One**

away from the senses — from a world of dreams
he has been here before
he is more than he seems

he is a traveler
nothing less —
nothing more —
e'er looking for the open door

on the path — his journey from a world unreal
always seeking the real deal

each day the same — different cities — he comes — he goes
forever searching for the **Love of God** for him to know

each day his sojourn ————— alone ————— there is one
every town —
every village —
always rising with **THE SON**

with **Christ** inside his being he travels along his way
living with the **Love of God**
throughout the entire day

# THE TRAVELER

I am a traveler of both time and space with visions I call my dreams
not confined by any place or anyone it seems
my mind expands into my soul with my body standing by
**GOD's** love and grace fill me so while others around me hide

they know not what they say or do as they stumble along the way
**Master's** words and thoughts fill my place each night  and every day

I trust my life with **His** care == I know just what **He'll** do
**He** slows me down from my race and turns my black to blue
**He's** in my mind most all the time with thoughts of love and joy
giving me answers to my questions **He** opens up the door

**He's** always here that I know == **He** never leaves my side
it is for me to be aware and never from **Him** hide
I love **Him** so == this I know I'll never turn away
**He** gives me more than I can know each night and every day

**He's** always here == **He** helps me grow == **He** shows me what is real
I cry and laugh in my race == my moments with **Him** I steal
now I go with the show of this I call my life
as long as I stay with **Him** == **He** will guide me with  **His** light

# COMMOTION

# society

the possessiveness of the illusions

==== seeks the self to **please**

## a disarray of living =========== people on their knees

forever going nowhere ============ wandering  through their day
gathering all they can get =============== thinking that is **The Way**
believing greed has only answers ========== forever wanting more
never considering what is real ========= never looking for the door

they come and go all about == with their pride they scream and shout
about the madness they think is real

never understanding **The Real Deal**

filled with worldly pleasures  ============ feeling they have it all
finding themselves empty =========== they wonder why they fall
drowning in a sea of darkness === never reaching a distant shore
always going nowhere================ forever looking for more

sustaining their contusions =========== in their souls they suffer so
never going inward == never gonna know about what really matters
no confusion about this one

always in the dimness of THE DELUSIONS ============== never finding the **Son**

UNTIL YOU CONFRONT YOUR

KARMA

YOU WILL BE CONSUMED BY IT

# MAYA

within the **Grand Marquee** of existence
it is easy to become lost
the illusions inviting all the senses
but it comes at a cost

detached from what really matters
enthralled by the world all around
so focused with life so illusive

the meaning of **God** still can be found

being center with all inside you
is what you're looking for
to escape from all the rumpus of life
you need to find the open door

away from everything around you
of your body you are no more

when you open up the magic of **God**
with the **Spirit of Christ** inside you
your life will soar

## Seconds

seconds to years ========================================= they go by fast
being happy in the moment is where it's at

no need to drift lost and confused
BUT it's a path many will choose

this semblance of reality
easy to behold
they walk like sheep and do what they're told
being happy on **GOD's** wonderful land
holding onto their gladness that is so grand

others among us will take a different stand
they learn to know and understand traveling daily along this land
feeling life is more than this == they look inside for the eternal bliss

**it is all on how we get along** == we can sing harmony in **The Song**
for those who may not know the tune
in their lives it may be too soon === **BUT** === it is ok == we're all on the way
going in our day in what we do **today**

# Let GOD's Love Light Shine The Way

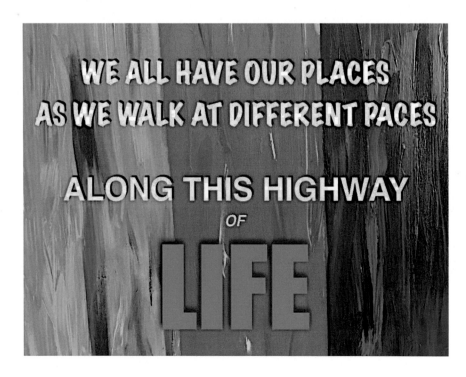

## the sea

the ocean is wide ==== the water deep
**the starless night gives fright**
**to all those that might navigate the forgotten seas**

forever going shore to shore
never knowing anymore than the waters they travel on
humanity a mystery
everyone running in **their day their way**

with **Master** I find in my mind the time to lift my spirit up
I have so much to do == for **Him** I sing my song

my **ego** and **fear** that some hold so dear
only get in my way and they're gone

I need the strength to give **Him** thanks == **He** takes away the fears
this is the way I walk today == with **His** love and guidance for the rest of my years

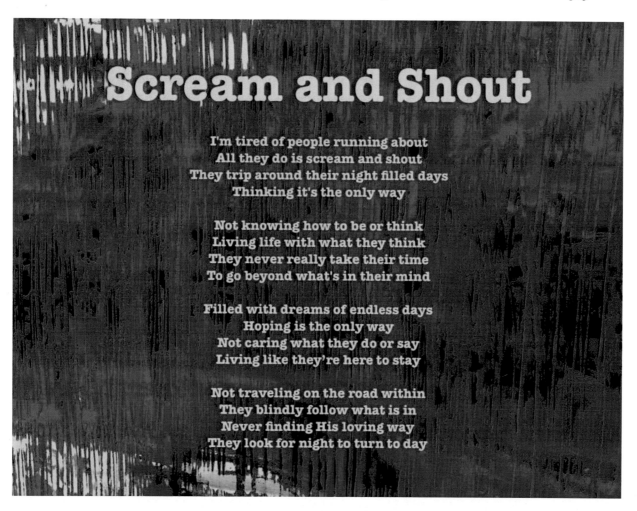

**Scream and Shout**

I'm tired of people running about
All they do is scream and shout
They trip around their night filled days
Thinking it's the only way

Not knowing how to be or think
Living life with what they think
They never really take their time
To go beyond what's in their mind

Filled with dreams of endless days
Hoping is the only way
Not caring what they do or say
Living like they're here to stay

Not traveling on the road within
They blindly follow what is in
Never finding His loving way
They look for night to turn to day

# TIME

early?
late?
what is **time**?
is it yours?                     is it **mine**?

running in front?
                          or falling **behind**?
          ——**f l y i n g   b y**?——
                          OR
                          staying in **mind?**

**ALL WE HAVE**
                          what time is late?
**LEFT IS TIME**
                                what time is **fine**?
                          do you get your time to **mind**?

                    OR
do you always run **behind**? === forever chasing but you never **find**
    always standing in the **line** forever looking for more **time**

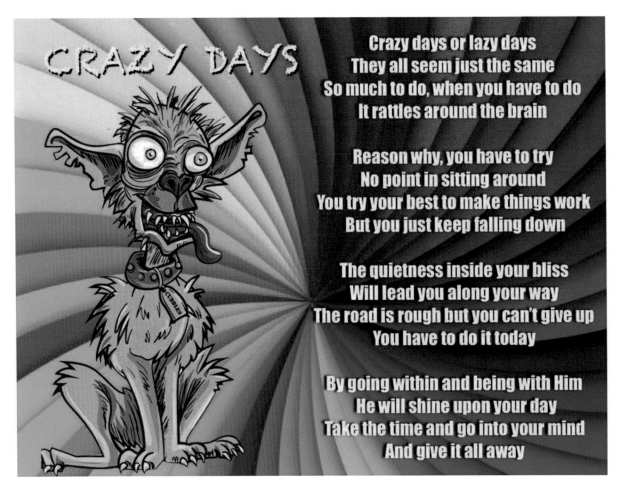

CRAZY DAYS

Crazy days or lazy days
They all seem just the same
So much to do, when you have to do
It rattles around the brain

Reason why, you have to try
No point in sitting around
You try your best to make things work
But you just keep falling down

The quietness inside your bliss
Will lead you along your way
The road is rough but you can't give up
You have to do it today

By going within and being with Him
He will shine upon your day
Take the time and go into your mind
And give it all away

# STAND TALL

are you dizzy when you're busy? == do you have so much to do?
so focused in your daily life == do you wonder what is true?
do you touch **God's** space and go with **Him** with inner harmony
or do you run at such a pace that you forget to see?

do you start each day on your way with heartache and wonder why
or heed **His** cry for LOVE and GRACE and stand by **Master's side?**

WITH love and understanding **He** will get you through it all
hold **Him** in your life and you will stand tall
LIFT your soul into **His** song and see where you can go
**with Him growing in your heart His LOVE for all to know**

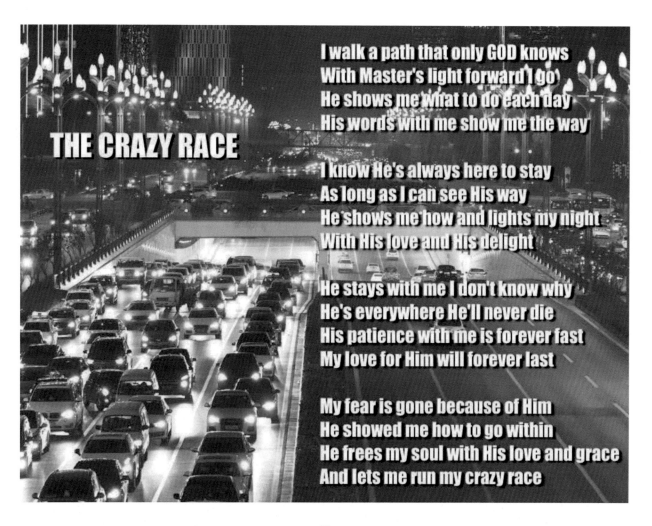

THE CRAZY RACE

I walk a path that only GOD knows
With Master's light forward I go
He shows me what to do each day
His words with me show me the way

I know He's always here to stay
As long as I can see His way
He shows me how and lights my night
With His love and His delight

He stays with me I don't know why
He's everywhere He'll never die
His patience with me is forever fast
My love for Him will forever last

My fear is gone because of Him
He showed me how to go within
He frees my soul with His love and grace
And lets me run my crazy race

# DUALITY

I am —————— I am not
I remember —————— I forgot
knowing nothing —————— only wise
knowing truth —————— hearing lies
finding somewhere is for sure
with **Him** is the **cure**

meaning nothing —————— finding all
going everywhere —————— within the same walls
knowing fake —————— accepting real
**always seeing is the deal**

going in —————— going out
talking quiet —————— shout it out
being happy —————— feeling sad
**ONLY WITH HIM AM I GLAD**

I am living - from **within**
loving all - and only **Him**

broken legs —————— dancing days
doesn't matter —————— meaning all

I can find **Him** from **within**
knowing **Her** - knowing **Him**

forever knowing - remember so
what I found - where I go

8

## Tomorrow

people running in and out == saying words they know nothing about
rushing in life is the way they know == without carrying on how they go
forever finding themselves in a race is the way they live their pace

it's not the way it needs to be

with **Master** you will find truth and understanding

not just words you hear but everything to hold so dear
**He** will set you free

go in
go out
say nothing == no need to shout

**His** light can change your night to day
not just words to say
it is the way to live the day == finding the path without the sorrow

**He** makes it clear == **He** whispers in your ear
you can learn to live that way today

AND TOMORROW

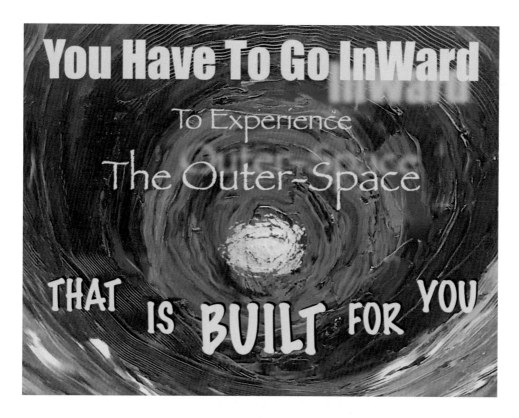

# doors

they =================
================= open
they close ============
================= do
you =================
================ really
know ================
================ which
way =================
================= the
direction ============================================================ ?
                                                                      S
                                                                      E
                                                                      O
                                                                      G

sometimes ==========
============ swinging
sometimes locking ====

**always** doing =========
nothing shocking =====

## most of the time

when it
sticks and doesn't work
you force
==================== a
way ================
==================== to
MAKE ===============
=================== it
open =================
and keep your journey going

not knowing how the hinges hold or how the lock got **broken**
you look for other ways

## to get the door open

*Sow The Seed Today*
*For The Tree*
*You Want Tomorrow*

# WAL | LS

they grow within —— they grow without
they become a barrier to shout about

why not try to get along?
let's all sing a different song
understanding where others stand and their journey across this land
and
finding truth within ourselves
not hiding lies or concealing the delusions that are dealt

LIVING LIFE IN EVERY WAY
being with all == **GOD** finds the way
happiness will forever stay finding **LOVE** in the day

living —— loving —— life should be
**HAPPY JOYFUL HARMONY**

GOD IS NOT ANGRY
DON'T FEAR HIM
LOVE HIM

# + POLARIZE -

the leaders of these lands take a stand with thoughts
that hide and misunderstand the hopes and the needs of the many
with desires of getting plenty of what they already have at hand

our nations divided =============== | =============== taking the side of the few
they wish to pursue
hoping to get more
of what they adore
with selfishness and greed

their delusions they create are not what we need

their words say plenty
so many don't have any
of the things our leaders have

words that divide =====|=====|=====|===== in them they
hide

what they really mean
they go on with their songs of selfishness and greed

let's hope the leaders
don't cause a lot of bleeders
with their politics of selfish greed

## Words

words can be misleading
actions are more true
the way you are going
you do the things you do

meaning often empty
words said here and there
doing is saying plenty
it shows how you really care

the reasons are many
you're lost and confused
not understanding
it's inside of you

the world we travel
is way too fast
it is words with meaning
that are gonna last

make no further promises
it's all inside your head
words without real meaning
rather not be said

We Don't Want To Hurt People
With Our Words
BUT
We Don't Want To Be Victims
Of Their Misalignments

# The Feudal Kings

we live in a **Feudalistic** society
where **Greed** has become the **King**
to his love and glory
the masses sing

dazed by the thrill of the moment ====== never grasping meaning within
they creep along in bewilderment ================ living with what is in
their days are empty =================== **lost** with confusion is **Their Way**
they **grope** through life and into the night === **stumbling** through the day
never finding any real meaning ======= **The ILLUSION** they think is real
**hoping** their lives are something ===== never finding **THE DEAL**

then at the **final** moment
they realize their life was UNREAL
**lost** in all of the confusion ========= their reality that they FEEL

looking for **The Show** at every moment == traveling blindly along the way
never withdrawing inward == just going about their day

embracing the delusion all around them == never seeing what is **true**
groping for all the worldly treasures == their **reality** they construe

life has so much more meaning
**GOD's** truth is all around
if you can get through the traffic ============== and not be bound to the town

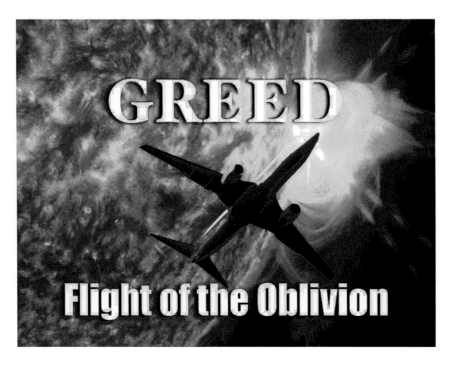

14

# PRIDE

within our ego the pride becomes alive into something unreal
it tears us apart away from **GOD**
and all that **He** reveals

it's within the pride that we hide — dancing in the **Grand Marquee**
away from **GOD** the ego thrives
with pride making it be

do all that you do
it's inside of you
you have so much more you can be

if you go the way
to find that day
you are forever free

in all that is around
**the love of GOD and CHRIST can be found**
IF YOU GO INSIDE TO BE WITH HE

DREAMS AWAKE

## noise

the noise inside my head reverberates
=========================== its vibrations tampered by the morning **Kriya glow**
**His** love inside of me =============================== my inner spirit knows

today's bloody battle has caused the red to flow
it is in my pranayama **His** light shows
all that is around me burns to the ground
with **His** love inside me my spirit can be found

today the battle is lost ============== the cost is severe
tomorrow we will take the field again knowing **His** love is near
it's in **His** daily lessons +++++++++ you will want them more and more
with **His** love and understanding you can find the open door

tonight the campfire glows ======= I will forget about my sorrow
with **His** love I will know and find **Him** here tomorrow
in a world all by myself I stand at **Masters** side
all the love and joy **He** gives me == I will never hide

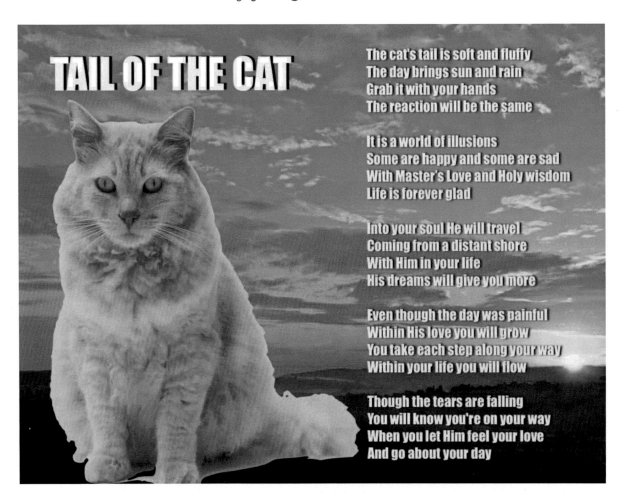

TAIL OF THE CAT

The cat's tail is soft and fluffy
The day brings sun and rain
Grab it with your hands
The reaction will be the same

It is a world of illusions
Some are happy and some are sad
With Master's Love and Holy wisdom
Life is forever glad

Into your soul He will travel
Coming from a distant shore
With Him in your life
His dreams will give you more

Even though the day was painful
Within His love you will grow
You take each step along your way
Within your life you will flow

Though the tears are falling
You will know you're on your way
When you let Him feel your love
And go about your day

# CONTRACTED

people get contracted in their daily dance
forever going nowhere
thinking life's a chance

not understanding or knowing when to let go
AND GO WITHIN
to do without is like a sin

hold **His** hand and go with **HIM**
let go of the breath and go within
**to know GOD's LOVE from within**

THIS IS WHERE IT CAN BEGIN

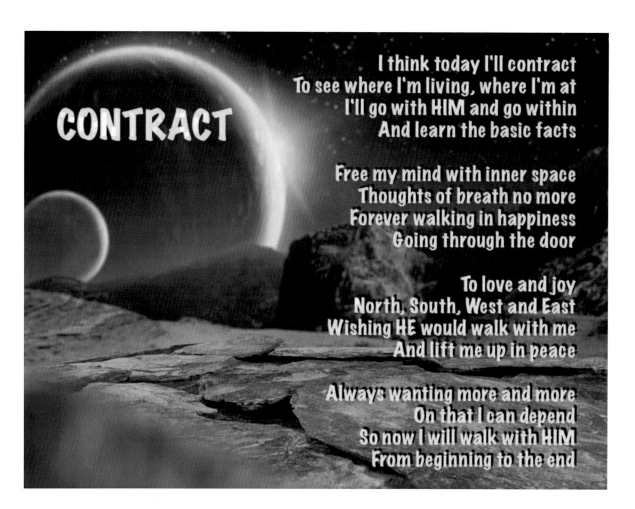

CONTRACT

I think today I'll contract
To see where I'm living, where I'm at
I'll go with HIM and go within
And learn the basic facts

Free my mind with inner space
Thoughts of breath no more
Forever walking in happiness
Going through the door

To love and joy
North, South, West and East
Wishing HE would walk with me
And lift me up in peace

Always wanting more and more
On that I can depend
So now I will walk with HIM
From beginning to the end

## chains

your attachments that bind you =========== won't hold me down
though I miss you ===================== you're no longer around

the words I told you and the things I do
you looked at them sideways
                              then you construed

a reality within you ====== much different than me
no longer bounded by your reality

chained to the world around you and all that holds you down
though I miss you == I'm glad you're not around

these words **He** tells me == I have so much to do
I'm sorry you're limited to who you think you knew

                              BUT
          there is so much with **He**

                              ======= of all the things I can be
your karma no longer blames me
                              ======= I am ready to be free

no more illusions that you hold so dear
I am not alone
I have no fear

the strength that's inside me
**God's** light does grow
alone on my path
with **Him** I will go

though you forsake me ================= it is your way
I look for **His** light to show me my day

I know we will go forward ============== to be who we be
but now I fly upward with **He**
================================= in my reality

# LINEAR

we live a linear existence —— it is how we be
what we do this very moment makes a difference to you and me

what is good is often plenty ————————— we take it as it comes
when the road gets rough and bumpy ——— we can smooth the path **within one**

the nighttime need not be fearful
no need to be so tearful
let YOUR consciousness r i s e

into the **higher realms**

awareness **within** begins with **Him** in the house where **He** dwells

days to come ————— there are many
we only know what we have done
to go inside and find **He** —— the mind becomes as one

into a higher awareness we find the spirit goes
what we do this very moment =====
**GOD'S LOVE** grows

the daylight battle is looming —- we can only guess what is ahead
to act and think in daily harmony with words **Master** often said

**the worldly lunacy is not what it is to be**
**life is so much easier when you walk with He**

the evening storms — they still do come
a deluge every day
with **Master's Light** on your path

you can find your way

**The Shore**

when pain and loneliness are at my door — it is **Master I look for**

lost and confused in the sea of untruths == **He** gives me the answers that cut me
——————————————————— loose

**He** shows me how to go within and let my spirit rise up with **Him**
THE BATTLE OF LIFE is here today
and will be here tomorrow

**He** lights my path along **His** way
today ===== tomorrow
without the sorrow

though I always walk with **Him**
I pray **He** will always let me in
today I travel in this world so fast
in my life **His** love will forever last

## DRUDGERY

the road of drudgery breeds in our minds
it's there that it gets its time
it doesn't exist == it's not around
then we give it clearance and it gets off the ground

entrapped in a feeling breeding within
by going within it all then begins
the foolish consistency that existed so grand
is no longer all around ============================= it's done with its final stand

the path becomes light == you know what you found
when you travel with **TRUTH**
you get off the ground

now is the day == only one thing to do

## IT'S TO FOLLOW THAT PATH AND TO THYSELF BE TRUE

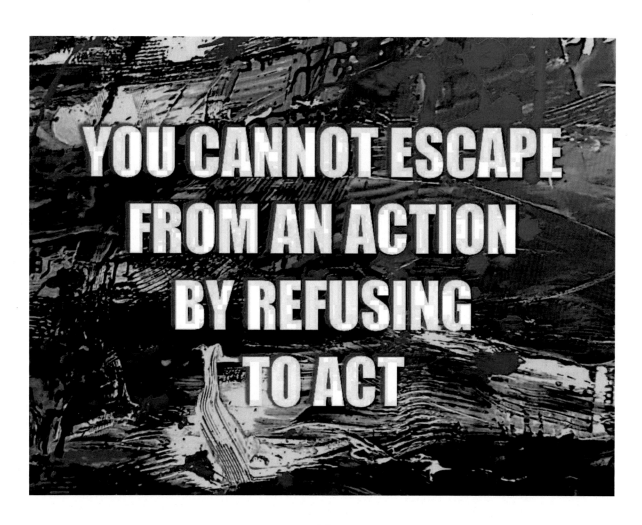

21

## compassion

we don't always get what we want == **GOD** always gives us what we need
though no one else is around == **Master's Love and Spirit** can set us free

**He** can come and help you in the darkest night
**He** can fill your life with happiness and delight

**He** can give you all the answers to everything right
if you let **Him** in your life

much joy and harmony you will find in all that is around
even on your last day **He** can show you the way on a path so bright to be found

**His Love Light** will fill you in the day and throughout the night
when you walk **His** way
**He** will bless you with delight

if you only let **Him** in
then you will find you begin
to understand long lost forgotten ways
**He** will help you get through your night and find harmony in you day

# running late

if we run late
we can still concentrate
on the way to go today

FREE from deceptions from the past that keeps the soul tied down

FREE to find **God's** joy and peace with **Master** as we run around

by finding **God's** love with **Him** and centering  spirit within

## time will be forever found

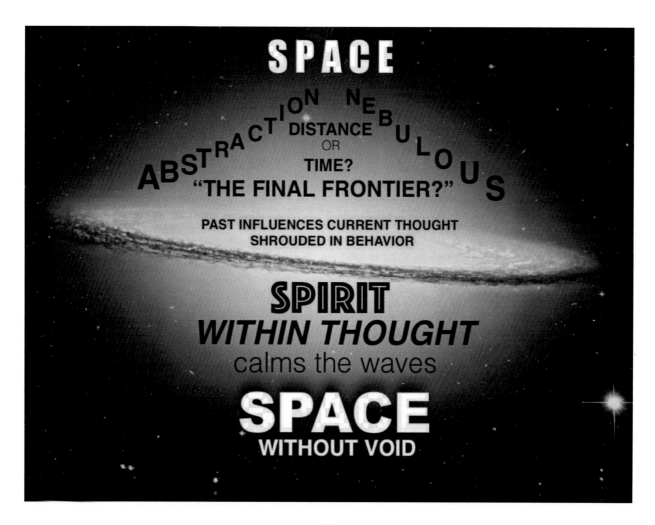

## The Storm

# A STORM REIGNS IN THE DARKEST DAY

we  look for **His light** to show us the way
the sea is rough ——— the waves are high
sometimes we can only lay there and cry

the mainsail is torn
the crippled ship carries on — crashing through the tempestuous briny deep
the meaning from **Him** comes from within
shows us the right path to keep

the crew is gone ................................................................. but the ship travels on
into the vociferous fury
the port is near — the storm is severe
the ship pounded by the waves — merciless and dreary

will tomorrow bring a rainbow of light to show **GOD'S LOVE** and endure the fight
or will the mainsail snap ......        ...... will the ship be too late
and succumb to the blustery might?

the rain is hard     we don't go far
into the deadly force
**He** pilots the ship
into the violent storm
**He** steadies the course

with all the sails tattered —
will the ship slip into the raging s
e
a

or will we find a way
to make it through the day
to mend its fractured hull?

# HE

steers the ship right ——————————— out of the dreadful fight
knowing the port is near
with **Him** at the helm — the ship won't be overwhelmed

# WE WILL FIND THE PORT AND BE FREE

# LONELINESS

**WOMEN**

women to my left ============  ============ women to my right

in the middle I sit and wonder
knowing **Master** is right

awake find my perception ...... it's okay to be this way
**He** grows **GOD'S LOVE** inside me

**His** light is in my day

at times I do get lonely ... it's nowhere that I go
only walking left and right
it's **God** I want to know

being in the moment is a good place to be
you will find true love and understanding by using **Master** as key

it is in **His** daily lesson ==== **He** shows us how to go
**His** truth and comprehension with all **God's** ways to know

**Soliloque**

Each day I stand
On this land
With You beside me

It is with Thee
That I be
From You I no longer hide

You give me the way
To walk each and every day
With Your Love inside that grows

I am free
To be who I be
With Your Love
For all to know

## Love Me Tomorrow

**GOD's** radiance illuminates me == reflecting on the path I go
——— is she there for me to know?

going hand and hand will we make a stand with what **Master** knows?
I'll see her tonight .... it will be alright .... in **His** light we will know
what of tomorrow? .... I will feel no sorrow
with **His** love we grow

will she cast her light my way and travel with **Him** and me?
will **His** eminent beam disseminate within our being?
will she play her heartstrings in my life and give it new meaning?
will our love become a ray of **GOD's** salient gleaming?

**GOD** ONLY KNOWS
along **His** way we will find the way to life's true meaning

## THE PATH

I met her today on **Master's** way == along the path of **His** shining
her beauty and grace is ahead of the race == is she here to find me?

**as I sing this song I never will go wrong**

                    I wonder if she has her mind on me?

not knowing when I will see her again
I hope someday she finds me

                    now I go alone in my home
                with truth and wisdom my mind on **HE**
                        I know this way is real
                                and
                    will stay that way forever

will we sing the same song? == I don't know how long until she knows it's me
both our stars shine bright == I don't know if she might even want to find me?

    now is today == we both walk the same way == I hope **Master** wants we
            I know I'll find out == I won't have to shout

        we're on the same path that finds **HE**

MOCKINGBIRD

How can she resist that song?
The one that he sings all day long
Knowing only right from wrong
Not flying in the air of confusion

Living only for the day
Is the only way
They know

Not caring how from why
Only wanting to stay high and dry

Singing in the air
And living life in union

## A Midnight Serenade

on a moonlit night we meet
with our spirits conjuring we can't be beat

we both bring much love and joy == we share it differently
we walk along the highway fast == free with **GOD's** reality
tomorrow's road == we don't know where
something special for you and me
our lights to shine in the moonlight night

A NEW QUASAR FOREVER BE

I know the times will VARY
worldly persuasions will visit us
with our love and understanding

IN **GOD'S LOVE** WE WILL TRUST

our flames will burn brightly == a crimson sky above the campfire glow
with **Master's Holy Wisdom** our love will flow
there's so much we both can be
if we help one another by using **Him** as key

**carcass**

she hangs out in the darkness == crying over a carcass from times of long ago
she can only find that time left in her mind when she was put behind and used up
years ago

she cannot grasp visions vast == what things can really be
instead she stays in her darkest days

someday I hope she's **f r e e**

now my wings fly far == I seek the stars

being so much more with **GOD**

**He** only knows

going forth with much to show == **Master's LOVE** sets me free
it is **His** life that makes things right and makes me be

with **Him** here the infliction I can bear == for **Him** I would do most anything
lifting my heart **He** makes my life restart == **He** brings me harmony

into another night with **His** light so bright with misery all around

**He** shows me how to go right now with **GOD'S LOVE** that I have found

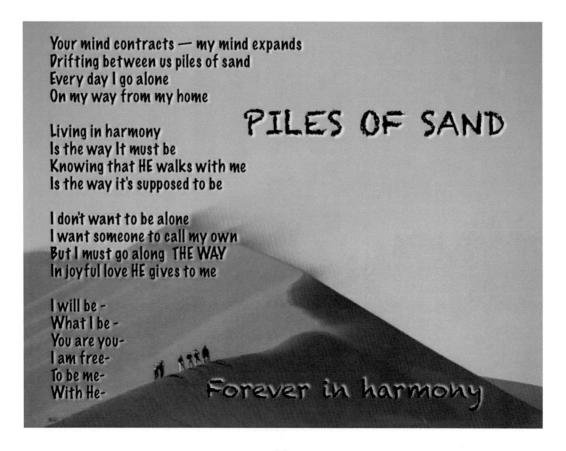

Your mind contracts — my mind expands
Drifting between us piles of sand
Every day I go alone
On my way from my home

**PILES OF SAND**

Living in harmony
Is the way It must be
Knowing that HE walks with me
Is the way it's supposed to be

I don't want to be alone
I want someone to call my own
But I must go along THE WAY
In joyful love HE gives to me

I will be -
What I be -
You are you-
I am free-
To be me-
With He-

Forever in harmony

# NOT ALONE

**Master** and me
that's how it shall be
knowing **He** will never leave me

## ALONE

**He** pleases me
knowing I will never be

## ALONE

**He** stays the night
**He** calms my fright
**He** shows me I'm right
when I follow **His** light

## ALONE

today is a day
like every day
when without **Him**
I would be

## ALONE

from deep within
the message from **Him**
I will never be

## ALONE

**alone**

the cost of life can be sever
                  **His** words and dreams make it clear

knowing which way to go — there is a door
                       but the journey is far
                       and filled with ropes and bars
                            they get in the way

on **His** path I stay
================== my spirit finding **His** light
alone there is **one**

far away I died == I know the reason why == still I try
                       **He** shows me why
                       these tears I cry

        **Master** guides me
                I no longer hide

**His Light** is so bright in a night filled with screams
**He** shows me how to walk right now == **He** fills my life with unknown dreams
I will find the way to get through this day == to sing **His** songs from my heart

    **He** is with me now == **He** shows me how to overcome life's challenges

there will come a time
=============== with **Him** in my mind == my body will be dust
                   but
        it is not now ========= I cry and try
          I know where I'm at

I'm **NOT ALONE**

**worry**

what is worry about?
it's something inside

==== makes you want to **shout**

what has happened = unfortunately so = with love and forgiveness

let the feelings **GO**

truth and wisdom from **GOD's** glowing rays
will get you through the haze
of useless emotion that goes nowhere
with thought and understanding you know you care

the sunrise comes tomorrow though the night seems long
with love and comprehension you'll sing **His** song

you know **Master** won't forsake you knowing you're aware
as you go onward ============================ in your daily affairs

# PAIN
# AND
# SUFFERING

# AGING

with **God** in mind
you will find that your time
becomes sublime

when your body hurts and you feel like dirt
time becomes more fine
with **God** in mind than without **Him**

though the days may seem dark and confused
you will always be right
with **Him** in mind you never lose

no longer blind
you will find
the happiness and joy of being divine

# He

will set you free
from your misery

when you walk with **He**

you will be

# THE BEST YOU CAN BE

## ALL RIGHT

the **pain** is so great
you cannot co n cent rate on anything you're doing

you're wondering where to go
==== is the world worth pursuing?

why are you suffering so?
you want to know
as each step you go hoping if wii be your last
is your life past?

only **GOD** knows

**HE** lets you know you're really OK
you're on your way finding the day and screaming through the night
pain lights it bright but **NOT** with fright

this you know because inside you **Master** grows

wanting you to know it will be **all right**

### Shout

in the silence == in the darkness == with nothing else about
I stand at the top of the stairs and all I can do is shout

cold, cold night is all that I feel
I look to **Thee** for warmth in all that is real

living here on my own ======= standing tall with **You** alone

my body is tired and in much pain
but
there's a fire inside my brain

what I learned from **You** == that I know
brings warmth within like the camp fire aglow

today == each day == I move along
looking for answers and singing new songs

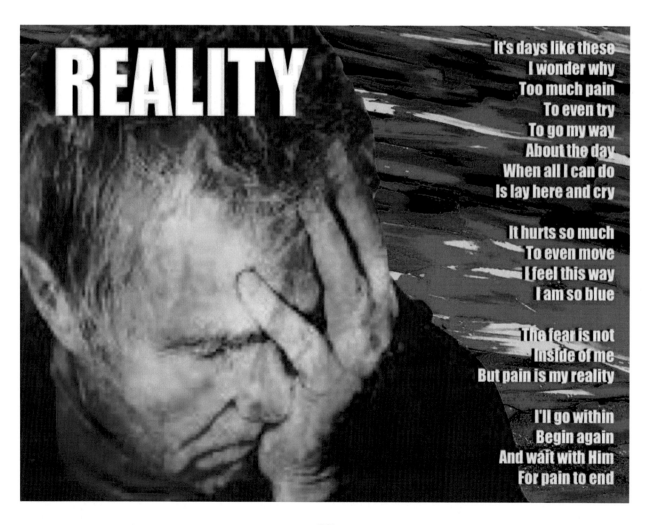

REALITY

It's days like these
I wonder why
Too much pain
To even try
To go my way
About the day
When all I can do
Is lay here and cry

It hurts so much
To even move
I feel this way
I am so blue

The fear is not
Inside of me
But pain is my reality

I'll go within
Begin again
And wait with Him
For pain to end

# TENSION

the lines of tension run through the darkness of life
it fills the mind with misery and keeps us from delight

finding the daily answers
in all that there is right
will help the body and mind to heal
with harmony in life

the screams no longer need to come == the body and mind set free
when you find the way today
============================================================= with this reality

unwinding the tension from within
you find the time in life is easier

if you do it with **LOVE**

# Today's Opening

no worldly way here today
going for days with the gaze of **ONE**
the pain so real
**He** helps me deal
**His** LOVE inside my brain

days come and go
in what they be

free
with GOD'S LOVE
my reality

I go in ——————————————— I go out
I shout it out
THERE IS SO MUCH MORE TO BE
**WITH HIM I'M FREE**

I TRAIN MY BRAIN
THE DRAIN REFRAINS

I SPEND
MY TIME            GOD LOVES ME
WITH HIM I FIND
ALL THAT I AM

**WITH GOD'S LOVE**

MY MIND FINDS        GOD LOVES ME
MY SOUL DEVINE

**INSIDE ME**    GOD LOVES ME

GOD LOVES ME    **I FOREVER SHINE**

GOD LOVES ME        GOD LOVES ME                    GOD LOVES ME

**I am with HIM**
**I am sublime**

GOD LOVES ME

37

**attachments**

they're here ————- they're there

# they're everywhere

like roots through soil
and dust in the wind
================================================= always attached to something
trapping us in the perplexity of the illusions
filling life with confusions
                   enabling one to misconstrue what is real

       finding long lost answers from within to without
     knowing  how to focus on what **MASTER** talks about

           living == loving == everywhere
          at journey's end you pay the fare
        going through life with too many cares
          by hanging onto attachments

ATTACHMENTS EVERYWHERE

We're grown to our attachments
They're almost everywhere.
Tying us to happiness
In things so wrongly cared.

They travel deep within our lives
And hold us down unknown.
They grow each day in our way
Like the dust that's in our home.

We laugh and cry in our days
In all that holds us down.
Only finding inner space
What is real is what we found.

Life's too short to waste away
On illusions so unreal.
Lift your soul into His grace
HE will help you heal.

# WHAT THE WORLD NEEDS NOW

## a cold night

winter's chill embraces a steady rain == the fires burns deep inside the brain
the spirit rises into a world of joyful bliss == the **Kriya** flows along with this

**MASTER'S** words and wisdom from long ago will introduce you to
HIGHER REALMS

these times are hard == they always are == it doesn't matter
**His** spirit goes far
traveling daily in the universe around
with **His** love inside us == **CHRIST** can be found
though conditions severe == have no fear

**He** has more to do for others who want the truth
to open **The Door**

**His** words are real == **He** helps the soul to deal
away the suffering each day == **His** love and joy lights the way
when you let **Him** in your life **He** will love you both day and night

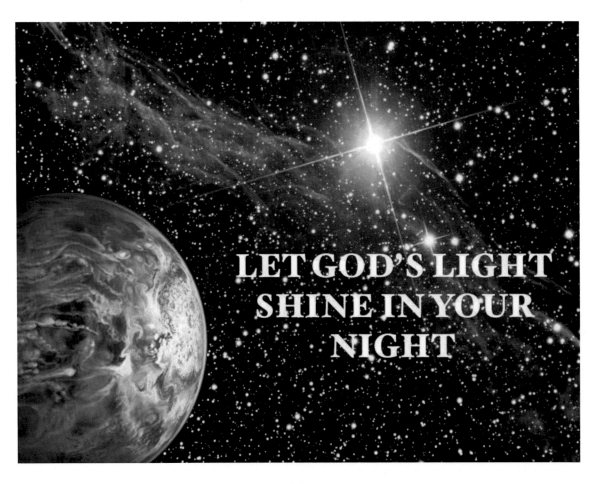

LET GOD'S LIGHT
SHINE IN YOUR
NIGHT

# illusions

from moment to moment

a life of dreams

exists within my being

an illusion ——— d r i f t s  in from the sunset sky
hiding the brilliant light

**Maya** blows from the west a winter storm
conspiring with **illusions** to become a reality

I seek the path **HE** is to show knowing only that **HE** is real

## NOT AN ILLUSION

now the roses grow
and I am to know
this God-given show
above the confusion

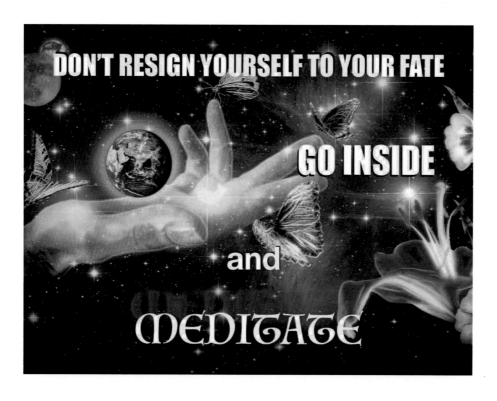

the suffering from the deception can be so grand
the self can no longer make **The Stand**

there are answers more and more == no need for misery
there is another door

you can find where it's at
**Master** is HERE — **He** will set you free

your will
**His** power
**His** light
**HIS LOVE**
will enlighten thee

if you seek **Him** more and more **He** will open all the doors
it is within that you begin by walking with **Him** the key
the feeling is right ========== it begins to show

### His Light of Love for all to know

to show the way
to walk the day
when you go with **GOD**

# Escape

this world escapes me
it's nowhere I want to be

I go within
to be with

# GOD

these times are tearful

alone

in the world

the pain is too much ===================== **the truth unfurled**

everyone                    is                    elsewhere

no one is here

alone

in this cold dark world

this vision is ugly

**I live**

**with Master I find**
**the truth and beauty**
**of His mind**

after this time == I am no longer bound == NOT having to travel
alone in the town

I can go away ======================= from the show
I s p e n d  m y  t i m e with **Him** — then I know

there is a **P E A C E**
that comes from the East
**His** path on this world
**SHINES  B R I G H T**
**HE WILL FILL  YOU  WITH  HIS  LOVE  AND  HIS  DELIGHT**

## From Within

no longer confined by four walls
visions within tell me it's OK ==
I'm finally on the way on a path known from the past

of where I've been
of where I'm going
of all I'm knowing
========= and growing within

love and understanding guide my way
no more clouds hiding the light from the day
I know this is the way because **Master** shows me
from within

constantly changing == forever rearranging
as memories fade **His** light shines the way

it's more than OK== it is **HIS** way of showing me
from within

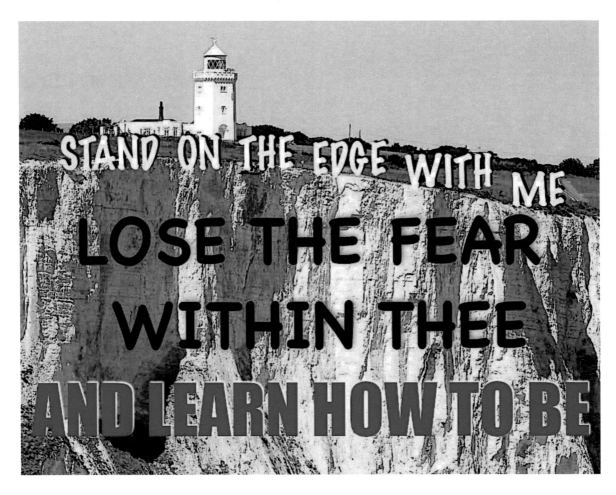

# silence

the silence is loud == **Master** shows us how **GOD** wants for us to be

don't hesitate
just concentrate
on **Him** for you to see

it is the way to walk today
with **Master** in your life
you are free

**He** gives us much more
than we could hope for
**GOD'S Light** that cures misery

**He** shows us the way
to live our day
with songs in our hearts in harmony

**He** can guide one and all
along the way
then all of mankind will be free

## My Song

**armed with the provision of THY grace**
================================= I walk these streets of fear
**YOU** travel with me in both time and space
================================= forever **YOU** are near

I think of **YOU** most all the time
================================= on **YOU** I can depend
**YOU** are always singing in my mind
================================= my song will **never** end

I stand strong  most all the time
================================= with **YOU** beside my side
the winds of change are in the air
================================= **YOU** are forever on my mind

**YOU** help me swim against the seas
 ================================= of heartache and despair
**YOU** lift my soul with **THY** love and grace
================================= **forever** and **everywhere**

**YOU** help me shine and grow strong
================================= into the hurricane eye
grant me knowledge of **THY** love
================================= to **thrive** with internal sight

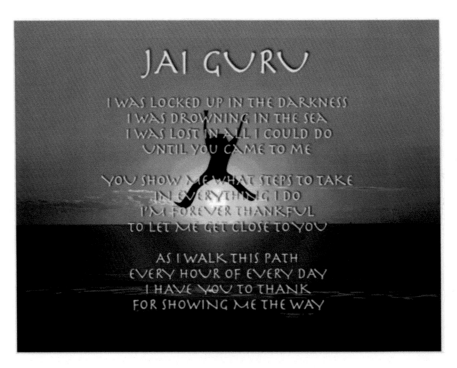

JAI GURU

I WAS LOCKED UP IN THE DARKNESS
I WAS DROWNING IN THE SEA
I WAS LOST IN ALL I COULD DO
UNTIL YOU CAME TO ME

YOU SHOW ME WHAT STEPS TO TAKE
IN EVERYTHING I DO
I'M FOREVER THANKFUL
TO LET ME GET CLOSE TO YOU

AS I WALK THIS PATH
EVERY HOUR OF EVERY DAY
I HAVE YOU TO THANK
FOR SHOWING ME THE WAY

# Highways

there's a place within your mind that opens to a universe beyond it all
there you will find a space where freedom will lift you and your soul will soar tall
away from the hurt == free from the distress of the world in which we go

in the comfort of your mind you will find the place where truth will be unfurled
and you will know

it's a route within the soul
escaping from the burning of the madness of the town
there you will find a light within yourself and all that is around

it's the wisdom that grows within  ======  feeling that you been here once before
only knowing where you been
you seek **His light** to find the open door

with **God's** light within
then with  **His** love you will begin
finding contentment within

===================== it's a feeling that grows =====================

the tempest storm rages all around
==================================== a way from the malady forever found
the real meaning of life is still around
free from the delusions most every day == the eye of the storm shines the way

free from the suffering that is all around **THE ONENESS** inside is forever found

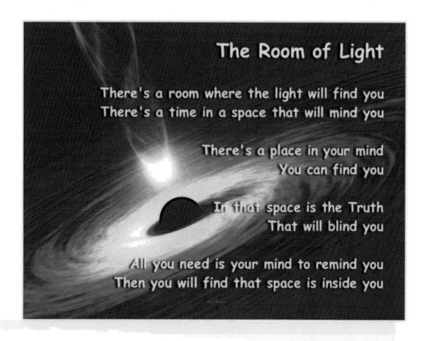

The Room of Light

There's a room where the light will find you
There's a time in a space that will mind you

There's a place in your mind
You can find you

In that space is the Truth
That will blind you

All you need is your mind to remind you
Then you will find that space is inside you

## The Master's Path *

the madness in the world burns all around the mind
attachments that run deep each day ================ travel with us over time

those days are empty ————- lost ———— and diluted as life can be

with knowledge of **His** words and **Holy** wisdom === we **are free**

**Master's** love and understanding travels with us within our minds
the struggle is hard  - there is so much to do - this land filled with illusions
with **His light** we see what is **true**

finding all inside us ——————————————————— this path we travel on
with **His light** guiding the way
we never will go wrong
at times these days are tearful ... we will not be fearful ... ALL THE SUFFERING
CAN BRING US DOWN

TAKING THE TIME TO GO INSIDE  — it is there **GOD** can be found

c a l m n e s s  inside the storm — **His eye** is always true
**He** gives our life new meaning.— it's for **Him** you want to do

the day brings many battles — some are won and some are lost
to know **God's love** and understanding — it's worth the final cost
the morning cold and darkness — another day begins

with **His light** in our life — we are with **Him**
though the days are not easy............ pain and confusion a l l  a r o u n d
**Master** gives us hope for tomorrow with **His light** the world will be found
today the battle turned bloody............ BUT ............THE WAR WILL NOT BE LOST

knowing **Cod** is with us ——————————— **He** thaws the morning frost
now we must travel forward  == into the day we go
with **Master's love** and understanding
# His Way For All To Know

*"Concentration on spiritualized thoughts in meditation actually eradicates the causes of the mental diseases and corroding bad mental habits. In meditation the mind becomes interiorized and withdraws the externally activating life force from the muscles and nerves and concentrates it in the brain cells where the evil tendencies are recorded. This concentrated life energy in meditation burns out the "grooves" or patterns of mental habits that are lodged in the brain". **The Second Coming Of Christ—The Resurrection of Christ Within You**, Paramahansa Yogananda p413. Licensed by permission of Self-Realization Fellowship.

# EPILOGUE: You Came To Me

**You** came to me when no one else would
**You** stayed with me through my bad and good
I slept so long === I thought it was a dream
=== years ago **You** warned me with a scream

I ran away === I didn't listen then
I was too scared === I thought it was the end
**You** stayed with me in my darkest days
=== as I searched the room for the light to turn night to day

**You** lifted my soul into **HIS** grace and made my limbs grow strong
as I take each step of this race === my song to **You** grows long

I don't know how I go my way === without **You** here both night and day
I'll walk with **You** to the end === **You** fill me so and let my life begin

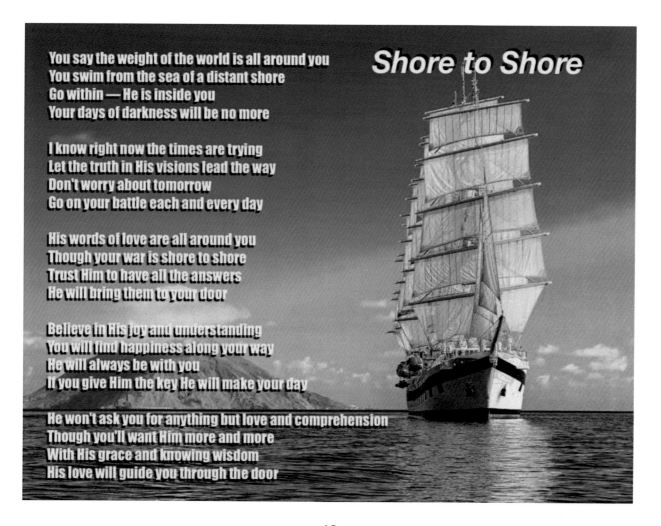

You say the weight of the world is all around you
You swim from the sea of a distant shore
Go within — He is inside you
Your days of darkness will be no more

I know right now the times are trying
Let the truth in His visions lead the way
Don't worry about tomorrow
Go on your battle each and every day

His words of love are all around you
Though your war is shore to shore
Trust Him to have all the answers
He will bring them to your door

Believe in His joy and understanding
You will find happiness along your way
He will always be with you
If you give Him the key He will make your day

He won't ask you for anything but love and comprehension
Though you'll want Him more and more
With His grace and knowing wisdom
His love will guide you through the door

**Shore to Shore**

# Temple Contact Information*:

Self-Realization Fellowship

3880 San Rafael Ave Los Angeles, Ca 90065-3219

www.yogananda-srf.org

Telephone (818) 549-5151

# PHOTOGRAPHIC CREDITS

## PAGE

COVER by Kent Thomas 1. Portrait: Guerrier Sandwichien by Nicolas Eustache Maurin, Public domain. Background by S _Photo, Shutterstock license. Composite by author. 6. Character by Anton Brand, Shutterstock license. Rainbow Swirl Background by Freepik, Creative Commons, Composite by author. 7. Creative Commons. Modified by author. 10. License by Pexels. Modified by author. 14. Background NASA photo credit 15. Dawn over Oostende-retouched, by Hans Hillewaert, Creative Commons 3.0, Modified by author and character by Kent Thomas. 16. Original images by Pxhere and Pexel CCO. Composite by author. 17. By S_Photo, Shutterstock license. 20. Composite by author. 22. Graphic art and canvas print by Kent Thomas. 23. NASA photo credit. Modified by author. 24. Rough Sea With Ships by Ludolf Bakhuizen, Public domain. Modified by author.26. Original photo By Bowen Pan , Edit by Cavit Erginsoy, Licensed by GNU Free Documentation/CC. Modified by author. 27. Photo by Charles J. Sharp. Creative Commons 3.0. Modified by author. 28. By Zolotarevs, Shutterstock license.30. Graphic art by Kent Thomas. 32. Statue photo by Purshi. Creative Commons. NASA Credit. Modified and composite by author. 33. Photo By Belight, Shutterstock license. 34. Background-NASA photo credit. Image by Kent Thomas. Composite by author. 35. Pixabay free image. Composite by author. 37. Stars NASA photo credit. Composite by author.38. Public domain. Modified by author.39. NASA photo credit for both images. Composite by author.40. Pixabay license. Modified by author. 41. Moon by Charles Lam, Creative Commons 2.0. Composite by author. 43. By Erik Gronnestad, Shutterstock license. Modified by author.44. NASA photo credit. Modified by author. 45. Background by FotoGuby, Shutterstock license. Composite by author. 46. NASA photo credit. Modified by author. 48. By Alvov, Shutterstock license. Modified by author.

## an **AFFIRMATION**
### to **FLY**

I awoke this morning
**F L Y I N G**
no chains holding me down
**GRATITUDE** filling my soul

FREE each day
going far
serving
is the way

INDEPENDENCE
being with GOD

# I AM FREE

**THY** will
not mine

one with DIVINE SPIRIT

I AM FREE TO BE ME

the ego
is
**LOS**T as i serve in **GOD**'s Holy Name

**I AM FREE TO BE ME**

everything that is
is inside of me

**GOD'S LOVE and JOY**
flowing through me

# I AM FREE

I will go forward ——— this I am sure
it is only with **HIM**
**I AM FREE TO BE ME**

no confusion in my earthbound ways — **HIS** light shines through my gaze
I AM FREE TO BE ME
serving others to relieve their pain and misery
**HE** shows me **HIS LOVE** —— I will never be the same
in **GOD'S HOLY NAME**
**I AM FREE TO BE ME**

## About The Author

Kent Thomas is a survivor. He was a successful physical therapist for 27 years living in Phoenix, Arizona until after suffering life threatening injuries from severe burns and head trauma , he participated in what is called pain management in this country. For over ten years he was under medical supervision of several doctors that managed his pain exclusively with pharmaceuticals. He was on a high dose of both opioids and benzodiazepines during that decade and had a stroke, underwent several surgeries and was rendered bed bound for 3 and 1/2 years due to the effects of both the injuries and the deleterious medical supervision that he was given by trusted authorities. He developed a debilitating disease called lymphedema and his body swelled, making even minimal physical activity nearly impossible. His weight grew to almost 400 lbs. He became lost in the darkness that surrounded him, made worse by the people he trusted that became his tormentors and exploited him. On a morning of sever darkness he became aware of a presence of an essence of light that was a spiritual awareness telling him there was another way. That life consciousness was the SPIRIT of **Paramahansa Yogananda.** It was at that moment his life began to change.

After three years of strenuous effort with skilled physical and occupational therapist, losing 150 pounds and getting off of the medications with the help of **God** and **Guru,** he is now a thriving member of the community and is has become an artist, poet, singer/songwriter and a devotee of **Paramahansa Yogananda.**

Printed in the United States
By Bookmasters